Little Lambs

# Ruth and Naomi

by Karen Williamson

Illustrated by Sarah Conner

CANDLE
BOOKS

Ruth lived with her mother-in-law, Naomi.

They had a hard time finding enough to eat.

"I'll return to my own country," said Naomi.
"Perhaps they have more to eat there."

Naomi was from the town of Bethlehem,
many miles away.

But Ruth didn't want Naomi
to travel on her own.
"Where you go,
I will go," she said.

"Your people shall be my people.
Your God shall be my God."

So Ruth and Naomi set off
together on the long
road to Bethlehem.

They arrived at harvest time.
Farmers were gathering grain.

"Go to the fields,"
Naomi told Ruth.
"Hungry people
can pick up grain."

Early in the morning,
Ruth went to a field.
It belonged to a farmer
named Boaz.

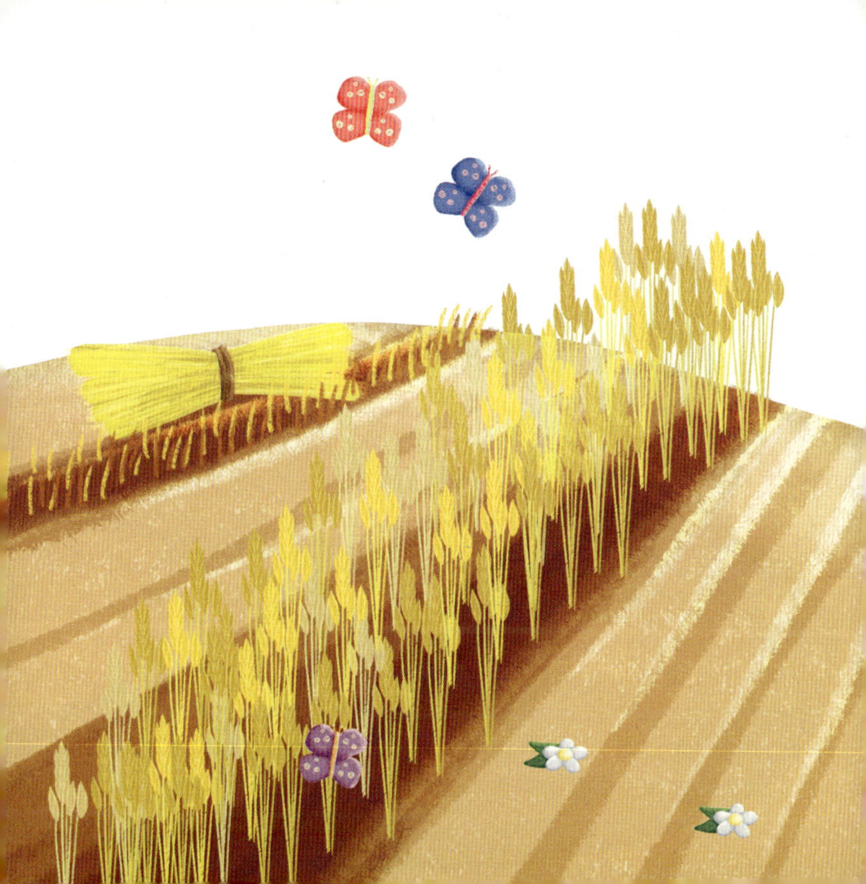

"Who's that girl?" Boaz asked a helper.

"Her name is Ruth," said the man.
"She's picking up grain to share
with her mother-in-law, Naomi."

"Be kind to Ruth," Boaz told his helper.
"Leave extra grain on the ground for her."

Some helpers shared their lunch with Ruth.

Ruth went home
to Naomi with a
basket full of
grain.

"You've done very well!" said Naomi. "Boaz has been kind to us."

Ruth returned to Boaz's fields every day
till harvest was over.

Boaz made sure all his
helpers were kind to her.
She always had lots
of grain.

Boaz had fallen in love
with Ruth.

Soon Ruth and Boaz were married.
"Please come and live with us," they said
to old Naomi.

Before long Ruth and Boaz had a baby.
"Thank you, God, for caring for our family,"
they said.